BROADCASTING IN SWEDEN

Other volumes in this series include

'Broadcasting in Peninsular Malaysia': Ronny Adhikarya
                                       with Woon Ai Lang,
                                       Wong Hock Seng,
                                       Khor Yoke Lim

'Broadcasting in Canada': E.S. Hallman
                          with H. Hindley,
                          R. Blackwood

BROADCASTING IN SWEDEN

Edward W. Ploman
with Sveriges Radio

CASE STUDIES ON BROADCASTING SYSTEMS

ROUTLEDGE & KEGAN PAUL
London, Henley and Boston
in association with the
INTERNATIONAL BROADCAST INSTITUTE

First published in 1976
by Routledge & Kegan Paul Ltd
39 Store Street,
London WC1E 7DD,
Broadway House,
Newtown Road,
Henley-on-Thames,
Oxon RG9 1EN and
9 Park Street,
Boston, Mass. 02108, USA
Manuscript typed by Vera M. Taggart
Printed and bound in Great Britain
by Unwin Brothers Limited,
The Gresham Press, Old Woking, Surrey
A member of the Staples Printing Group

ISBN 0 7100 8529 X

interesting work is being carried out by scholars in several countries on promise and performance. These studies are not so ambitious. They are designed to provide easily accessible information about a wide variety of cases (including cases where market forces are the main influence on what happens) and to cover big and small and old and new countries alike. The first cases chosen include some where there is no existing manageable monograph and some where the experience of that country is of particular general interest at the present time. As the series unfolds, there will be increasing scope for comparison and contrast, and international patterns will doubtless be revealed - of 'models', 'imports' and 'exports', and of regional 'exchanges'. If it is likely that such comparison and contrast will become more sophisticated than it has been in the past, it is at the same time certain that it will be of increasing value in the future to those policy-makers who are concerned to frame their choices clearly and to see their own circumstances in perspective.

Meanwhile, the International Broadcast Institute, which has sponsored this series, will continue to concern itself also with the general opportunities and problems associated with the continuing advance of communications technology. The Institute is an international body which seeks to bring together engineers and social scientists, lawyers and programme-makers, academics and administrators.

The author of each case study in this series has been free to assemble and present material relating to his own country in a manner decided upon by him, and he alone is responsible for the evidence presented and the conclusions drawn. Yet guidelines have been given him about arrangement and coverage. Thus, he has been encouraged to ask such questions as what have been the critical points in the history of broadcasting; how has that history and the broadcasting structures which have evolved been related to the history of other forms of communication (the press, for example); what are the main institutional relationships at the present time; what are likely to be the future trends; and whether it is possible to talk of an integrated 'communications policy' in that particular case.

The International Broadcast Institute as an institution has no views of its own on the answers to such questions, but its trustees and members believe that answers should be forthcoming. Much of the serious study of communications systems has been carried out within the confines, cultural as well as political, of national boundaries, and it is such research which most easily secures financial support. This series will point in a different direction. It is not only comparison and contrast which are necessary but a grasp of what problems and opportunities are common to countries, not necessarily alone but in the great continental broadcasting unions or other groupings.

We can now trace the beginning of a 'global' sense in communications studies. Indeed, the word 'beginning' may be misleading. The sense certainly long preceded the use of satellites and was anticipated in much of the nineteenth-century literature. The world was being pulled together: it was becoming a smaller place: everyone everywhere would be drawn in.

Communications policies have often, of course, pulled people apart in clashes of images as well as wars of words. And some of the case studies in this series will show how.

Two final points should be made. First, nothing stands still in communications history and there are bound to be changes between the writing of these case studies and their publication. Second, because the British case is at present under review, treatment of it in this series is being deferred. Meanwhile, the first three studies come from three different continents and some of the structures are the newest of all.

Asa Briggs
Chairman, IBI Research Panel

INTRODUCTION

How does any broadcasting system really feel - to itself
and to its audience? The facts, regulations and statistics in the following study can only give part of the
picture. The specific meaning and relevance of broadcasting and the density of reaction to radio and television obviously depend on particular features in each
country. The images on Swedish television screens resemble, to a large extent, those in other countries. Why,
therefore, did Ingmar Bergman's 'Scenes from a Marriage' -
which when shown on British television resulted in not
much more than a polite yawn - cause such a stir in
Sweden?

   There are a number of reasons why an account of broadcasting in Sweden should include an analysis of what it
is to be a Swede. One observer has said that one of
Sweden's outstanding, though not particularly useful,
achievements has been an ability to stimulate a highly
varied panorama of reactions. But such an approach, however tempting, would go beyond the scope of this study.
None the less, it is worth pointing out that compared to
most European norms, the specificity of Sweden is not only
one of geography and climate but also of social and political development: over a large surface there is a small
population with an unusual degree of ethnic and cultural
homogeneity, a recent history without wars and revolu-
tions, a late but then rapid industrialisation and urban-
isation, and a legal system that is neither civil nor
common.

   Not that this has made for less debate or confusion
about broadcasting than elsewhere. As with other things
Swedish, stability and change are layered in a specific
manner and certain constants characterise the development

and character of Swedish broadcasting.

A first striking feature is the rapid growth of broadcasting which seems to have filled a deep-felt need in Swedish society. Since the introduction of sound broadcasting any forecasts of, say, the increase in the number of sets, whether radio, TV or colour TV have always fallen short. Relative to population, growth has been extremely rapid and constant - until, recently, saturation levels started being reached.

Thus, the expression used in Swedish legislation about broadcasting occupying a central position in social life is neither a pious wish nor a boast. It is a fact. Indeed, we have reached the point where one might wonder whether Swedes do not take their broadcasting almost too seriously. They do not seem to spend the same amount of time listening and viewing as do the Americans or the Australians, but there are few countries where broadcast programmes so easily seem to become national events, not only with major ice hockey or soccer matches but equally with a quiz programme or a series by Bergman. And this happens in a country where the population has ample access to other media and to other means of education, culture and entertainment.

This central position is, in a somewhat ambivalent form, reflected in the relations between broadcasting and the press. There are few - if any - other countries where the press seem to devote as much space to broadcasting. Not one day passes without major national newspapers devoting entire pages to what often looks like minute goings-on at the Swedish Broadcasting Corporation. And in the popular periodical press broadcasting personalities seem to have ousted traditional stars.

A further interesting feature is that the Swedes, while muddling through their broadcast issues much like everybody else, seem quite happy not only to accept what to others would seem contradictions but cheerfully build them into regulations and structures. It is difficult to imagine a more non-Cartesian approach than the current regulations which provide for wide decentralisation and strong centralisation at the same time. Even having two competing TV channels under the same roof was not good enough: local radio recently became independent of, in association with, the main broadcasting corporation. Signs point to a similar paradox for the new organisation of educational broadcasting - perhaps even for broadcasting generally.

The interest shown by the public and the press in
broadcasting seems to be shared by the authorities. Even
though Swedes have been described as naturally and inordi-
nately prone to set up committees, inquiries and studies,
broadcasting and the media have recently received more
than a lion's share. To paraphrase the words of the present Director-General of Swedish Broadcasting, it is to
be hoped that broadcasting will not suffer the fate described in a famous Swedish saying: When the last Swede
dies he will do so suffocated by the dust from public
inquiries - into the last Swede.

Chapter 1

ENVIRONMENT FOR BROADCASTING

Despite its small size and relative unimportance as a
European state, Sweden has been examined and re-
examined by a host of foreigners who are anxious to
prove that Sweden is either a paradise or a hell on
earth. (Steven Koblik (ed.), 'Sweden's Development
from Poverty to Affluence 1750-1970', University of
Minnesota Press, Michigan, 1975.)

One reason for this variety of irreconçilable evaluations
might be found in certain features which are specific to
Sweden and when compared to other countries are seen to
provide a different physical and social environment for
broadcasting.

There is no denying that Sweden today tops a number of
international statistics, from life expectancy to newspaper reading (though not of suicide as is often alleged),
nor that it is seen as one of the most prosperous countries in the world. What is often forgotten is that as
recently as the mid-nineteenth century Sweden was one of
the poorest, most underdeveloped countries in Europe.
Few, if any, countries have gone through such rapid
transformation - amazingly, without violent upheavals. In
about a hundred years, from being poor, rural and agra-
rian, Sweden has become rich, industrialised and urban.
A hundred years ago, more than three quarters of the
population earned their livelihood from farming, fishing
and forestry - today less than 7.5 per cent. In 1900 only
30 per cent of the population lived in urban areas as
opposed to 70 per cent in 1960 and an expected 90 per cent
in 2000.

Admittedly, late industrialisation helped the country
to avoid the major evils of the 'paleo-industrial era' but
the swiftness of change shattered old patterns of Swedish

life. Barely had what looked like a combination of certain constant features and new patterns established themselves when, in the last decades, the moral and intel-
lectual climate changed into such new directions that
paradox became endemic.

1 BASIC FEATURES

With an area of some 450.000 sq.kms Sweden is the fourth
largest country in Europe. With only 8.2 million inhabitants the country has one of the lowest population densi-
ties (20 inhabitants per sq. km, compared to Italy's 185
and France's 96). However, the population is unevenly
distributed. About 90 per cent of the population lives in
the southern part of the country, but even so only the
areas around the three largest cities (Stockholm,
Göteborg and Malmö) have somewhat more than 50 inhabitants
per sq. km.

   It is therefore quite reasonable to characterise Sweden
as mainly a land of immense forests broken by some 96,000
lakes which make up 9 per cent of its surface area.

   Despite the geographical position - Stockholm is
roughly level with the southernmost tip of Greenland and a
large part of the country lies within the Arctic Circle -
the climate has been described as 'remarkably bearable'.
In fact, the country is only habitable thanks to the
Gulf Stream which flows past the coast of Norway and
brings warm air from the west. In northern Sweden there
is usually snow for six months of the year but further
south the winter is shorter and milder, so that in the
southernmost part there can be a growing season of some
eight months. The summers are relatively warm. The
'general contrast between light and darkness, between
warm, even hot summers and icy winters, is basic to
everything in Sweden and seems to affect all aspects of
Swedish life' (Paul Britten Austin, 'The Swedes', David &
Charles, Newton Abbot, 1970).

   The climate would permit many types of farming but
only 10 per cent of the land surface is arable while 55
per cent is productive forest land. The aim of the
agricultural policy is to maintain 80 per cent self-
sufficiency. As raw-material-based industries, especially
forestry, have declined in relative importance, the emphasis has shifted towards production of finished goods.
This shift towards technology-intensive products is even

more pronounced in the engineering industry which is able to use domestic supplies of iron and copper ore but also has to rely on imports for its requirements of raw materials. Engineering products now represent 40 per cent of the value added by all industries with pulp and paper in second place (14.8 per cent) followed by food processing (9 per cent), wood products (9.1 per cent), chemicals (8.7 per cent), iron, steel and other metals (6.6 per cent).

The low birth rate, the low mortality and the high life-expectancy have caused an unusual population structure: the over-65 age group now represents as much as 15 per cent of the population, the under-17s no more than 25 per cent and the productive age-groups, measured as those gainfully employed, some 50 per cent.

Over the centuries, Sweden has experienced little invasion and almost no immigration, which is mainly a recent, post-Second World War phenomenon. The Swedes have therefore been one of the ethnically most homogeneous people in Europe, and also culturally: the Swedish language is entirely dominant as was the Evangelical Lutheran religion.

This homogeneity has of course been taken as one of the reasons for the relative stability in Swedish political and social life. Equal importance is often given to the fact that Sweden never had a feudal system on the European model: the farmers remained free and the original Swedish Riksdag (parliament) from the beginning did not have three estates as in the rest of Europe but four, the farmers being the fourth estate.

A more recent explanation is the stability of the party system. There are five parliamentary parties in Sweden and it is extremely unlikely that their number will increase. Since the achievement of universal suffrage in 1918 the constitution of parties in the Riksdag has remained largely unchanged. Since 1932 the Social-Democratic party has remained in power, alone or in coalition with other parties.

2   CONSTITUTION AND ADMINISTRATION

Constitutionally, Sweden is a parliamentary democracy with the monarch as the ceremonial head of state.

Sweden's new one-chamber Riksdag has 349 members. The
Cabinet, which includes the Prime Minister, the heads of
the 13 ministries, and several ministers without port-
folio, takes collective responsibility for all governmen-
tal policy decisions.

It is characteristic of the Swedish parliamentary
system that most of the important work takes place in
standing committees whose members represent the different
parties on a proportional basis. However, Bills are prepared according to a peculiar system which some observers
believe leads to the Swede being represented twice over.
The cause is the active participation of the so-called
interest organisations in government and administration.
Most major interest groups in Sweden - industrial workers,
white-collar workers, professional people, farmers,
businessmen small and large, teetotallers, religious
sectarians, athletes, motorists, landlords, tenants, etc.
- have one or more national organisations to represent
them.

Where their interests are involved these organisations
are usually asked to sit on the commissions of inquiry
established by the Riksdag or by the government which pre-
cede almost any Bill. When these commissions have comple-
ted their reports, every conceivable organisation and
public or private body likely to have an interest in the
proposed reform is asked to submit its views. Only then
does the Ministry concerned prepare the Bill which is discussed in one of the standing Riksdag committees before
going to plenary and vote. This then is the manner in
which proposals for changes in the broadcasting system are
also handled.

Sweden has for centuries made a clear distinction between the functions of the ministries and the central
administrative agencies (or public service boards); law
is thus not implemented by a ministry but by these agencies which now number about 80. They have a constitu-
tionally-guaranteed independent position in relation to
the Government. In this respect the interest organisations often play a further role since they are frequently
represented in the decision-making bodies of the administrative agencies or in advisory boards associated with
them. Even if the Swedish Broadcasting Corporation has
been formally given the legal status of a limited company,
it in fact resembles one of those independent administrative agencies in the appointment and composition of its
Board of Governors.

By long tradition the Swedish civil service is apolitical. Except for top political appointees, the majority of civil servants employed in the ministries, numerically very small, and in the administrative agencies, enjoy security of tenure. They cannot be removed without trial but are, on the other hand, personally accountable since any civil servant may be sued for abuse.

A further safeguard against possible abuse of power at any level of administration is the provision 'on the public character of official documents' which is included in the constitutional law. This rule, which makes all public documents - except those defined in a special law - open to inspection by any member of the public, forms part of the Freedom of the Press Act and is crucial for the conduct of journalism whether written or electronic.

Another safeguard is the office of the Ombudsman. The first Ombudsman was designated in 1766 and the institution has been in existence continuously since 1809 and has served as the model for similar offices in other countries. The Ombudsman is elected by the Riksdag and is responsible only to the Riksdag. He supervises the application of laws and other statutes and acts as a watchman over potential abuses within the entire judicial and administrative system, both national and local - the only persons exempt are the King and the ministers, the latter being subject to parliamentary responsibility.

The institution of the Ombudsman has been extended in recent times. There are now Ombudsmen appointed by government for supervising trade practices and consumer protection. In the media field, there is a Press Ombudsman who does not have the status of a civil servant but is appointed by a special committee and proposals have been made for the establishment of a Radio Ombudsman.

If Sweden has an old tradition of centralised administration, she has an even older tradition of local government. The 24 counties to a large degree manage their own affairs through an elected County Council, even if in many respects they are responsible to the central administration. Each municipality also has a local council elected for a three-year term and is responsible and self-governing in local matters, primarily for public services such as road, water supply, sewerage, old age care, basic education, etc.

The independence of the judiciary is protected constitutionally. The judicial hierarchy resembles that of other countries, but Swedish law is based on old Nordic law with only a limited influence from Roman law or common law jurisprudence.

The stability of Swedish social life extends to the labour market. Most individual firms through their trade associations belong to the Swedish Employers' Federation (SAF) and up to 90 per cent of blue-collar workers belong to local unions, affiliated through their national associations with the confederation of Swedish Trade Unions (LO). In practice, the centralised negotiations between LO and SAF set the pace for negotiations between other labour and management bodies. Two institutions have contributed to the stability of labour relations. The Labour Court established in 1928 is part of the public court system and has exclusive jurisdiction over conflicts involving labour-management contracts. It includes labour and management representatives. The other is the voluntary Basic Agreement between LO and SAF signed in 1938 establishing rules and procedures for collective bargaining. Major issues on the labour market now are greater democracy at places of work and measures to increase the quality of the working environment.

Sweden is often called a socialist country. If by socialism is meant state ownership of the means of production this is certainly not true. Swedish manufacturing industry is owned 90 per cent privately, 5 per cent co-operatively and only 5 per cent by the state. In other sectors the co-operative movement plays a more important role: producer co-operatives account for 25 per cent in forestry, 80 per cent in agriculture, while consumer co-operatives have 20 per cent of the retail sales sector. There is though, at the same time, an unusual degree of co-operation and planning between the state and industry as well as a strong central government economic planning. The government plays an active role in promoting adjustment to business cycle fluctuations and structural changes, through employment, investment and regional development policies.

If by socialism is meant social welfare Sweden certainly fits the bill. In general terms, the aim of the social welfare system is to guarantee every resident of Sweden a minimum standard of living in certain specific respects such as food, living, education, etc. and to provide support in emergencies such as illness and

unemployment. Also, the intention is to redistribute
income more evenly over each individual's life cycle, to
narrow the gaps between different social classes and to
provide everyone with a broad range of social services.

   Since 1945 Swedish education has undergone extensive
reforms at all levels. The system now provides for a
compulsory nine-year basic schooling after which some 90
per cent of all young people aged 16 continue to the new
comprehensive secondary schools for two to three years
where they are offered 22 courses of study including
technical, economic, commercial and vocational training.
Instruction and textbooks are free. About 25 per cent
continue to higher education. Sweden also has a long
tradition of adult education in the form of residential
adult colleges and evening study courses which are
arranged by study organisations affiliated with popular
movements, political parties and universities. They
attract some 2 million adults each year i.e. about one
third of the adult population.

3 COMMUNICATIONS AND THE MEDIA

Telecommunications

Telecommunication services are provided and operated by
the Telecommunications Administration which is organised
as a central administrative agency and run as a public
commercial enterprise. It is headed by the Board of
Telecommunications consisting of the Director-General
and five persons chosen from outside the administration
and appointed by the government. The Swedish Telecommunications Administration enjoys, as do similar agencies such
as the railways and postal services, a greater freedom of
action than administrative agencies not concerned with
public commercial enterprise. But certain major questions
have to be submitted to the Riksdag or the government.

   The Telecommunications Administration is responsible
for public telephones, telegraph and telex communications,
both domestic and international, as well as for radio communications with ships, radio services for civil aviation
and the distribution of broadcasting programmes. A rapidly expanding field of activity lies in the provision of
data transmission via the telecommunication network. The
Administration is also charged with the management of the
radio frequency spectrum in accordance with obligations
under the International Telecommunications Convention and

it represents Sweden in the ITU conferences.

As a general indication of the development of telecommunications in Sweden, there are some 5 million telephones (including service sets) in use which means 633
telephones per 1,000 inhabitants which represents one of
the highest figures in the world.

Media

Swedes rank among the world's leading newspaper-readers.
The country has just over 100 daily papers with a circu-
lation totalling some 4 million copies, i.e. more than an
average of 1.5 copies per household daily. Daily papers
are published in some 80 cities and provincial centres
throughout the country. The growing concentration of
press ownership has led the Riksdag to pass a Bill providing direct subsidies to newspapers in economic
difficulties.

While Sweden has no mass-circulation weekly news maga-
zine, more than 4,000 magazines and other periodicals are
published, 40 of which circulate well over 7 million
copies per issue (in a population of 8.2 million). In
addition, there are about 1,000 parish bulletins, 270
school magazines and 270 house organs. Trade unions, professional organisations and similar special interest
groups publish a total of 500 journals, mostly of high
quality. There is one national news agency, the co-
operative Tidningarnas Telegrambyrå (TT).

The annual film production dropped from 30 feature
films in 1957 to only 15 in 1961, largely due to competition from television. Government encouragement, mainly
through entertainment tax relief and the establishment of
the Swedish Film Institute, has helped to raise annual
production. The Institute is financed through a 10 per
cent levy on ticket sales and gives general support to
feature film production and to a number of awards, and is
responsible for culturally significant activities (arch-
ives, training, research, etc.)

Chapter 2

EVOLUTION OF BROADCASTING IN SWEDEN

Regular sound broadcasts started in 1923 and were undertaken by a variety of radio clubs set up by individuals,
private interests and by the Telecommunications
Administration.

As early as 1924 the authorities decided on a basic
structure for broadcasting which has been maintained to
this day. Distribution and programming are handled by
different institutions. The state, through the Telecommunications Administration, was made responsible for
the establishment and operation of the transmission network, while the programme activities were entrusted to a
specially-created organisation.

The nature of this organisation was somewhat unusual.
Swedish radio was not given the independent legal status
of, say, the BBC nor was it made part of the national
administration as has been done in many other countries.
Instead the broadcasting organisation, A.B. Radiotjänst,
was established as a non-profit-making public corporation;
a limited company in which the radio industry held one
third of the shares, and the press and the Swedish News
Agency (TT) the rest. The main reasons for this seem to
have been the wish to ensure independence from government,
and to enable various interested parties to participate in
broadcasting. Moreover, the working procedures of the
public administration were not considered appropriate for
radio production.

Public interest was protected by the introduction of a
licence fee system for financing the broadcasting system
and by government representation on the Board of Governors.
The government concurrently laid down certain directives
on programme activities which provided a basis for the

objectives of Swedish broadcasting for decades to come.

It is interesting to note the early, close relationship between broadcasting and the press. The Swedish News Agency and Radiotjänst had the same managing director for ten years. It was also stated in an agreement between the Telecommunications Administration and the corporation that Radiotjänst was not to prepare its own news bulletins but that these were to be handled by TT.

In 1927, the government established a Programme Council, a body for the general evaluation of all Swedish broad-casting programmes. It was later abolished and some of its functions entrusted to a special complaints body.

Broadcasting in Sweden developed with extreme rapidity. After only ten years 700,000 licences had been issued, which meant that nearly every third household had a receiving set. Sweden immediately followed the UK and Denmark in numbers of sets per capita. Thus, in a rela-tively short time, broadcasting became one of the most important mass media in the country.

Its development has been punctuated by public com-mittees of inquiry - about one per decade. The Broad-casting Inquiry requested by the Riksdag (Parliament) in 1933 proposed the nationalisation of broadcasting. This was rejected and the Riksdag decided to maintain Radiot-jänst and the basic arrangement concerning the share-holders, but with a larger government representation on the Board of Governors.

The 1943 Broadcasting Inquiry proposed the introduction of a second radio programme, the extension of external broadcasts on short wave (which had been introduced during the war) and more broadcast time for adult education. Because of lack of equipment and labour during the war it was decided not to introduce a second radio channel but to extend the distribution network mainly through wired distribution.

In the early 1950s both the Telecommunications Adminis-tration and Radiotjänst raised anew the question of more programme channels. Proposals from a committee of inquiry set up in 1952 led to a series of decisions from the Riksdag in 1955. A second sound radio programme was to be introduced. The distribution was to be ensured through wire transmission in areas with inadequate recep-tion conditions on long and medium wave frequencies, and

through FM transmissions in other parts of the country.
The choice of FM was also motivated by plans for a television network.

Experimental television transmissions started in 1948
at the Royal Technical College.   Three years later the
1951 Television Inquiry Committee was established, which
presented its proposals in 1954.   Further legislation was
passed by the Riksdag in 1950, 1957 and 1958.

The most important decision was to adopt the same basic
structure for television as for radio.   It was to be financed through licence fees.   The concept of commercial
television was rejected.   Television programming was to be
handled at the national level by one corporation,
Radiotjänst.   The initial financing of television would be
through allocations from the surplus of licence fee payments.

This legislation also resulted in certain structural
changes.   The shares in the corporation were reallocated.
Press shares were reduced to 40 per cent, another 40 per
cent were offered to groups representing the popular movements and 20 per cent to organisations representing trade
and industry.   These proportions were later changed to 20
per cent for the press, 60 per cent for the popular movements and 20 per cent for trade and industry.   Since
broadcasting is a non-profit-making activity financed
through licence fees, shareholding should primarily be
seen as a method providing for a balanced representation
on the Board of Governors.   Along with these changes the
name of the corporation was changed to Sveriges Radio A.B.
(SR).

Because of the great popular interest in television the
distribution network was established much faster than
originally planned.   The number of licences issued by June
1959 was expected to be about 72,000 but was in fact more
than 400,000.

In 1960 a new Broadcasting Inquiry was set up.   Its
mandate was to investigate the future of sound broadcasting.   In 1962 the future of television was added to its
scope of inquiry.   This inquiry presented a number of proposals in succession which, with some changes, led to
legislation providing the basis for the present structure
and development of broadcasting:

1 In 1964 the Riksdag decided to extend a three-channel
   sound broadcasting network over the entire country,
   mainly on FM.
2 In 1966 the main legislation was adopted; these Acts
   are noted below in chapter 3.
3 In 1969 a second television channel was introduced;
4 In 1970 colour television was officially introduced
   and today most television broadcasts are in colour.

PRESENT BROADCASTING STRUCTURE

1 OVERALL VIEW

The operation of broadcasting in Sweden is thus divided between the Swedish Telecommunications Administration which is responsible for the establishment, maintenance and operation of transmission and distribution facilities, and Sveriges Radio, which has the sole and exclusive right of determining what radio and television programmes should be broadcast.

There are three national sound broadcasting programmes, mainly distributed through FM transmitters, with some coverage provided through medium and long wave and a short wave external service. The three national services are on the air for about 350 hours per week. Since 1966 there have been two television channels with a total programme time of about 100 hours per week.

Sweden now has a very high density of receivers per capita: radio: 383 sets per 1000 inhabitants; TV: 351 sets per 1000 inhabitants. As of December, 1975, the number of licences issued was: radio only: 230,275; radio/TV combined: 2,909,252; of which colour TV: 1,388,437.

2 GENERAL CHARACTER

There is broad agreement in Sweden that broadcasting is a service to the general public which must be performed in such a way as to satisfy the dual demands of independence and responsibility.

Broadcasting must be free in the sense of being

independent of both political and commercial influence.
The responsibility required in broadcasting is not only
expressed in the legislation relating to it but, because
of the general attitude towards mass media which has
evolved in Sweden, there is a social demand for a relatively serious programme output. This has often been
defined as the requirement of quality in terms of both the
proportion of serious programmes broadcast and the professional level attained by individual programmes.

Under the exclusive right conferred upon Sveriges Radio
there is also an explicit demand for a varied programme
output not only in terms of the scope of the issues and
subjects dealt with but also in terms of the responsibility to provide a broad, comprehensive and serious presentation of the widest range of subjects, opinions and
attitudes.

The general character and objectives of broadcasting
in Sweden cannot be understood except against the back-
ground of the special, in certain cases unique, legislation concerning freedom of expression, freedom of the
press, protection of news sources and access to public
documents.

The Swedes pride themselves on the fact that their
Press Law of 1766 was the first constitutional legislation in history providing a clear protection of the press
and of freedom of expression. The hundred-plus articles
of the Press Law are part of the Constitution, which
cannot be changed without the consent of two sessions of
Parliament with a general election in between.

Special features of this legislation are worth noting
as they apply to broadcasting and to a large extent
define what can and what cannot be done in programming.

Of fundamental importance is the principle that official documents are open to public inspection. All documents received by national or local authorities, or which
are drawn up by these agencies, are accessible to any
person whether directly affected by the subject-matter or
not. This rule applies not only to individuals, but to
the media as well. Exceptions are few, and regulated by
law. They concern military matters, relations with
foreign countries, and restrictions designed to protect
the integrity of the individual (for example, medical
and criminal records, etc.)

Another fundamental principle concerns the protection of the anonymity of news sources. According to the Freedom of the Press Act newspapers, and by extension radio and television also, are forbidden to reveal their sources even to the police or to a court. This Act, and certain other laws, also define offences against the freedom of expression, such as slander, libel, etc. This legislation is designed to provide lenient penalties for offences against freedom of expression. In a recent publication the system is defined as follows: 'The legal regulation of freedom of expression is so modest, so restrictive in interpretation and circumstantial in application that a more flexible, extralegal system has been created in parallel' (Lars Furhoff, Lennart Jonsson and Lennart Nilsson, 'Communication Policies in Sweden', Unesco Press, Paris, 1974). This generally takes the form of internal self-regulation - for example the codes of conduct adopted by the Swedish Publicists' Club which are applied not only by newspapers but also by broadcasting.

The Press Fair Practices Commission, sponsored by the Publicists' Club, the Newspaper Publishers' Association and the Swedish Journalists' Union, acts as a court of honour. There is also a Press Ombudsman appointed by a body which consists of the parliamentary Judicial Ombudsman, the Chairman of the Swedish Bar Association and the Press Co-operation Council.

In principle the modest legal limits to freedom of expression are the same for printed publications and broadcasting. The requirement of impartiality implies that broadcast programmes shall provide a reasonable balance between various interests and opinions and shall also endeavour to achieve within the public service broadcast system the diversity which unrestricted publishing rights establish for the print media. Sveriges Radio is at the same time, by virtue of this requirement, prohibited from favouring some opinions over others or from taking a stand of its own on issues discussed. None-theless the corporation is also enjoined to safeguard fundamental democratic principles, among them freedom of expression.

The application of these rules can sometimes resemble tightrope walking. There has been considerable debate about the manner in which these principles should - or could - be applied in the case of political creeds favouring a violent and thus unconstitutional change of the political structure.

At present new legislation on freedom of expression is being prepared with the objective being to replace the Freedom of the Press Act with a comprehensive law covering all the media.

New principles for public policy regarding the cultural field, introduced in 1974, are also applicable to broadcasting. These concern such general objectives as the equalising and improvement of the social environment, decentralisation, freedom of expression and the responsibility of social institutions to promote these objectives.

3   LAWS AND REGULATIONS GOVERNING BROADCASTING

(a)   General

The basic principles underlying Swedish broadcast legislation are:

1   The authorities decide the general framework for the operation and development of broadcasting through regulations concerning broadcast transmissions, the economic basis and the adoption of guiding principles for broadcast programme activities.
2   To ensure maximum independence on programming, programme activities are delegated exclusively to a corporation, in the legal form of a limited company, which enters into agreements with the state.
3   The double principle - national public service and independence - is intended to provide maximum freedom of expression; this is buttressed by the prohibition against advance censorship and the establishment of a body, outside and independent of the corporation, to examine programmes and handle complaints about programmes, after broadcast.

As mentioned above, the currently applicable legislation was adopted in 1966. It should be noted, however, that new legislation concerning local radio was decided by the Riksdag in May 1975, for application as from 1 January 1976. Moreover, a number of parliamentary and government committees of inquiry are still at work on various aspects of the mass media, including broadcasting. It is expected that there will be - within the next few years - further changes in broadcasting legislation. (More details are provided in chapter 6.)

(b)   Radio Act

The basic regulation is contained in the Radio Act of 30
December 1966. The main features are:

1 Broadcasting has been defined as including both over-
   the-air transmission and wire transmission; the main
   criterion is that transmissions should be intended for
   direct reception by the public with the exception of
   such transmissions intended solely for a closed group,
   whose members have a manifest community of interest
   other than just listening or viewing such transmissions (Art. 1).
2 Permission is needed to possess and operate a radio
   transmitter; such permission is granted by government
   or by an authority designated by government (Art. 2).
3 Anyone may possess and operate receivers; subject to
   approval by parliament, government may prescribe fees
   for the possession of receivers (Art. 3).
4 The 'sole and exclusive right' to determine which
   programmes shall be included in broadcast transmissions is to be conferred upon a corporation designated by government (Art. 5).

   Of special importance are the regulations stipulated
by the Act concerning programming. They are mainly of
three kinds, all expressed in very general terms:

1 The exclusive right granted according to Art. 5 shall
   be exercised 'impartially and objectively'; otherwise
   the exercise of this right shall be determined by an
   agreement between government and the designated corporation (Art. 6).
2 In Art. 8 there is an explicit prohibition against
   censorship, a provision of crucial importance.
3 Examination of broadcast programmes after transmission
   shall be the function of the Radio Council; detailed
   regulations governing the Council's work are decided
   by government (Art. 7).

(c)   Agreement between the government of Sweden and
      Sveriges Radio

Pursuant to Articles 5 and 6 of the Radio Act, further
regulation of the broadcasting service is set out in an
agreement between the state, represented by the government, and the designated corporation, i.e. Sveriges
Radio AB (SR). The main provisions of the Agreement
concern:

1   The obligations of the corporation in the exercise
    of the sole and exclusive right to operate broadcast
    programme services.
2   The division of responsibility between the corporation
    and the Telecommunications Administration.
3   The major organisational features of the corporation.
4   Basic programming policies.
5   Financial arrangements, including a prohibition
    against commercial advertising.

The various aspects and implications of these regulations
are analysed under chapter 3, section 4.

(d)   Broadcasting Liability Act

To align regulations concerning liability in broadcasting
with those applicable to the press, special legislation
was enacted in 1966.

   The abuse of free speech in broadcasting shall give
rise to liability and damages only when the offence is
one of 'broadcast libel', defined as the representation of
matter which would have been actionable as press libel if
committed by means of printed matter. Relevant provisions
of the Penal Code referred to in the Press Act are also
applicable in the case of broadcast libel.

   According to the Freedom of the Press Act, only one
person, the 'publisher', is held responsible in the case
of press libel. In view of the differences with the press,
the responsibility for avoiding libellous content in
broadcasting is vested in 'programme supervisors'. Such
programme supervisors are to be appointed, in accordance
with government regulations by the Director-General or
other officials of the corporation At present, 50 programme supervisors can be appointed.

   Nothing may be broadcast contrary to the decision
of the programme supervisors and no one else may be held
liable for broadcast libel. Liability for the indemnity
of injury is held jointly by the corporation and the responsible programme supervisor.

   The Act is supplemented by a Proclamation regarding its
application.

(e) Articles of Association

Since Sveriges Radio has been legally constituted as a
limited company, certain basic regulations are provided in
the Articles of Association in accordance with the Com-
panies Act of 1910, revised in 1944. It is recalled that
the shares have been divided between the major popular
movements and organisations, the press and organisations
in trade and industry.

The provisions for the composition of the Board of
Governors are given in the Articles, the main provision
being that the chairman and half the number of members and
alternate members are appointed by the government, the
other half by the general meeting, with two additional
seats for staff representatives.

(f) Regulations for the Radio Council

As with previous legislation, the Radio Act prohibits
advance censorship of broadcast programmes. Special procedures for complaints against programmes and examination
of programmes after broadcast had already been adopted in
1935. The current legislation includes provisions for the
complaints procedure through Art. 5 of the Radio Act and
the special regulations concerning the Radio Council.

The only duty of the Radio Council, an independent
public body, is to verify that the corporation exercises
its exclusive right impartially and objectively and in
observance of the directives for the programme services
laid down in the Agreement. For further information concerning the activities of the Council, see below.

(g) New legislation adopted in May 1975; stereophony and local radio

1 Following experiments with different systems for
stereophonic broadcasting, among them the Swedish developed FM/FM compounder system, parliament opted for the
internationally recognised pilot tone system. This system
will be introduced in all three sound broadcasting channels over a period of five years at an estimated cost of
Sw. Crowns 11 million (£1.0 million).

2 The new legislation concerning local radio implies a
decentralisation of the present sound broadcasting

structure to increase the opportunities for satisfying information requirements at the local and regional level.

The country is being divided into 24 local radio districts, each with their own management, an average staff of 14, and a transmission time varying between 10 to 15 hours a week. For this activity, a new organisation is being created as an independent subsidiary of Sveriges Radio, in which Sveriges Radio holds the shares while the government appoints the majority of the Board of Governors.

These local transmissions will, for the time being, be accommodated within the third FM sound channel. The implications for the national programmes of Channel 3 will be decided through a special agreement between Sveriges Radio and the Local Radio Corporation.

The establishment of this new corporation, which should be independent from Sveriges Radio, implies that the traditional exclusive right of Sveriges Radio to broadcast transmissions comes to an end. The reasons for this are to provide guarantees for a clear allocation of resources, the introduction of new, simple and rational journalistic and technical operational conditions, administrative simplification and a stronger position for local radio activities.

It is stated, however, that the main corporation, i.e. SR, shall be responsible for the overall planning of broadcasting, shall request financial resources and decide the general budget for the Local Radio Corporation, SR shall also decide on programme rules valid for broadcasting in general. As regards staff policy, the two corporations shall be regarded as one. Furthermore, SR shall represent the two corporations in negotiations concerning union agreements, copyright and neighbouring rights, as well as in negotiations with national institutions about sport, music and news.

Programming in local radio is to be decided locally and shall be geared to the coverage area. In local radio, much emphasis should be laid on programmes dealing with trade and industry, labour market conditions, education, popular movements and cultural life within the area. One of the main objectives for local radio should be to constitute a forum for a dialogue between municipal and other elected officials and the public at large. Moreover, attention should be paid to linguistic and ethnic minorities as well as to local educational programmes.

The investment cost has been evaluated in Sw. Crowns 34 million and operational costs in Sw. Crowns 47.8 million The new organisation is being introduced immediately.

This legislation has been mentioned in some detail, since it might, at least in part, serve as model for the future organisation of educational broadcasting.

4   INSTITUTIONAL RELATIONSHIPS

(a)   With government authorities in general

As shown by the afore-mentioned legislation, the relations between SR and the government differ at various aspects or levels of broadcasting. In the following, five of the most relevant aspects are analysed: general regulatory, programming, organisational, operational and financial.

General regulatory

1 It is recalled that according to the Radio Act, a corporation designated by the government has the sole and exclusive right to determine programming. The basic relationship between the corporation and the state is an agreement between the government and SR.

The current Agreement is valid for ten years (1967 - 77). Notice of termination must be given no later than a year before expiration, otherwise the Agreement is renewed automatically for five years. The only other possibility of terminating the Agreement would be a breach of the Agreement by the corporation. This must be established according to a special procedure, set out in the Agreement: the government can institute an inquiry in accordance with the Law of Arbitration; if the inquiry so warrants, the government may terminate the Agreement.

The basic regulations concerning the duties and activities of the corporation are laid down in the Agreement. In consideration of the sole and exclusive right to 'determine programmes to be broadcast', the corporation undertakes to operate broadcast programme services. In particular, the corporation is enjoined to produce or otherwise procure programmes, to employ required staff and to acquire premises and equipment.

The Agreement also provides the basic regulation
concerning the relationships between the corporation and
the National Telecommunications Administration, the Radio
Council, and the educational authorities. In summary,
these relations are regulated as follows:
1 the general policies and guidelines are laid down by
   parliament and government;
2 otherwise public authorities are forbidden to influence
   programme activities;
3 breaches of the Agreement by the corporation are dealt
   with by the Radio Council;
4 breaches against legislation concerning freedom of
   expression are dealt with by the courts.

2 The Radio Act includes only two tersely formulated but
fundamental provisions concerning programming: a basic
expression of the requirement for impartiality and
objectivity in programming (Art. 6); prohibition against
censorship (Art. 8). These complementary provisions
should be seen in conjunction with the regulations concerning the Radio Council and liability in broadcasting.

The prohibition against censorship is extensive. The
Act forbids any 'authority or other public body' to
examine broadcast programmes in advance, to prescribe such
examination, or to prohibit a broadcast or wire transmission on account of content.

This regulation, to safeguard freedom of expression in
broadcasting and more specifically the independence of
the corporation in programme matters, is aligned with the
provisions of the Freedom of the Press Act.

In practical terms, these regulations make it impos-
sible for the government to direct programming. Questions
in parliament or diplomatic representations concerning
individual programmes are rejected with a reference to the
complaints procedures, dealt with by the Radio Council.

Recently, SR sought an authoritative clarification of
the provision in Art. 8 of the Radio Act through a peti-
tion to the Parliamentary Judicial Ombudsman. The result-
ing statement by the Ombudsman not only maintains but
actually strengthens the position of the corporation in
its dealings with public authorities. The immediate
reason for this action was a television programme on personal damage during military service and the payments made
to those suffering damage in military accidents. The
military authorities has been prepared to co-operate in

the programme on certain conditions, which were regarded
as unacceptable by Sveriges Radio.

The Judicial Ombudsman stated that it would not be in
accord with the principles of freedom and independence of
the press and broadcasting that this freedom be 'contrac-
ted away' through an agreement that a journalist accepts
to respect the indications of an authority concerning
deletions or changes. The authorities should not even try
to get SR to agree to anything but should act with regard
to the freedom and independence for broadcasting laid
down in the Radio Act. The Ombudsman also pointed out
that the Chief of the Army seemed to have supposed that
an authority having participated in an interview could
decide if and how that interview should be broadcast -
when in fact it is the responsible programme supervisor
who decides while the participating authority may present
observations. Thus, the authorities acted against the
law when they requested the programme to be broadcast
according to their instructions.

Programming

The Radio Act's basic regulation about programming policy,
only states that the exclusive right given to the corporation 'shall be exercised impartially and objectively'.
This regulation is supplemented with more explicit provisions in the Agreement. These are four main kinds.

1 SR shall concentrate on national programmes distributed
over the whole country; there is, however, an additional
requirement to make optional use of material and programme
opportunities in various parts of the country. The provisions concerning regional services have been superseded
by new legislation of May 1975, concerning local radio.
The corporation is also requested to produce special programmes for transmission overseas.

2 The basic policies for the general conduct and content
of SR programmes provide that: (a) the corporation 'shall
uphold the fundamental democratic values in its programme
services'. In application this provision has been taken
to mean that 'undemocratic' opinions may be included in
programmes but are not to be left without rejoinder.
(b) The programme services shall also be conducted with
regard to the central position of radio and television in
society. In the Agreement it is then stated that not only
is the corporation required, inter alia, to disseminate,

in suitable form, information on current events as well as
on important cultural and social issues, but also to
encourage debate on such issues (Art. 6). (c) Special
attention is paid to the requirement for diversification
of programmes in character and content: different interests and tastes shall, 'to a reasonable degree', be
satisfied as well as the special interests of minority
audiences (Art. 7). Of utmost importance regarding impartiality and objectivity are the provisions in Art. 8,
which supplement those of Art. 6 of the Radio Act. The
first requirement is that they should be applied so as to
ensure 'extensive freedom of speech and information shall
obtain in broadcasting' and, to a reasonable extent, 'an
overall balance between different opinions and interests'.
It should be noted that in view of the provisions of
Articles 5 and 8 of the Radio Act, the corporation has the
sole responsibility to decide how these principles shall
be applied and put into effect.

There is an additional requirement concerning veri-
fication of facts. The corporation is enjoined to verify
carefully factual statements in programmes prior to transmission, so far as circumstances permit.

These provisions concerning programme policies also form
the basis for possible action by the Radio Council, which
can only pronounce on whether SR has followed the basic
provisions of the Radio Act and the Agreement, and cannot
concern itself with other programme matters.

3 The Agreement includes a general statement that the
privacy of individuals shall be respected unless overriding
public interest dictates otherwise. Since, in the prepara-
tion of the entire 1966 legislation, it was not the intention to extend the definition of acts which might entail
criminal or other responsibility, this matter was not further elaborated. It is thus up to the Radio Council to
evolve adequate rules in this area.

Art. 8 of the Agreement also includes general provisions concerning correction and right of reply. This has
been complemented by internal rules adopted jointly by
the Nordic broadcasting organisations and has therefore
not been further included in national legislation.

4 Art. 11 of the Agreement gives a general regulation
concerning public announcements. For 'announcements of
importance to the general public', requested by a central
government authority, the corporation is enjoined to

permit their broadcast and shall ensure that the announce-
ment is in a form suitable for broadcast and does not prejudice the programme services by reason of length or
otherwise. This matter has been the object of considerable discussion in connection with the extended use of the
broadcast media for public social information in a more
general sense. (See comments below concerning the 1975
parliamentary discussion.)

Organisational

The relationship between the authorities and the corporation at the organisational level operates at two levels:
the legislative or other measures concerning the organisation of the corporation, and the membership of the Board
of Governors.

1 The Radio Act gives no indication of the organisation
of the corporation beyond stating that it should be
designated by government.

    In the Agreement, the overall organisation of the
corporation is laid down in Art. 4, which is supplemented
with certain directives formulated in the government's
proposal to parliament and in pronouncements by the relevant Parliamentary Standing Committee. These directives
have thus been approved by both government and parliament.
They provide for a management structure consisting of the
Board of Governors and the Director-General, and for six
independent programme units: radio, television channels 1
and 2, educational programmes, overseas services and
regional broadcasting. Also, there should be an engineering division. The directives give the heads of the
various programme units direct responsibility for their
service under the general supervision of management.

    It is significant that the directives state specific-
ally that each programme unit shall be allotted an overall budget within which it has the right to make its own
detailed dispositions. These budget appropriations should
not only cover salaries, fees to performers and other
direct costs, but also the costs of technical services,
accommodation, purchase and rental of programmes, films,
etc.

    Technical equipment and production facilities should,
as far as possible, be adapted to the requirements of the

programme service. It is foreseen that the heads of the
programme units will be able to influence the construction
and role of studio buildings as well as the choice of
equipment.

As the 1966 legislation was linked to the introduction
of a second television programme, particular attention is
paid to the relationship between the two television channels. The two television channels are supposed to be competitive within the framework of one organisation and each
should be given equivalent budget appropriation. The
management of each channel has the right to determine the
content of their broadcasts in terms of live or film pro-
ductions, programmes purchased from outside, relays from
abroad or freelance production. The directors of the two
channels should to a considerable degree be free to determine the organisation and size of their programme staff,
the policy for staff recruitment, etc.

One reason for the introduction of two competing,
largely independent television programmes under the same
roof was to defuse certain demands for a commercial channel. The aim was to achieve competition within the
existing system and to avoid what was seen as the negative
consequences of commercial television.

2 In view of the strong centrifugal forces, which have
been built consciously into the organisation, the directives stress the need for a strong management, which is
specifically responsible for maintaining common planning
for observance of the general policies laid down for the
corporation and for the operation being conducted with due
regard to the principles of economy and sound management.
However, in order to safeguard the intended independence
of the programme units, the directives state the common
planning and co-ordination should be confined to the allocation of transmission time in main categories, such as
news, entertainment, drama, etc. The intention is that
the opportunities of choice should be increased, but there
is no requirement for a rigid application of a 'contrast'
principle in programme scheduling.

There are some obvious limitations placed on the independence of the television channels and the other programme units. Competition in the transmission of major
public events, sports events, etc., is to be avoided. A
central common news department for 'hard' news is established as a service to the programme units, but they are

free to use other news sources and should concentrate
their output on commentary, analysis and reportage.

Other common services include the SR Symphony Orches-
tra, the purchasing of films and contracts with artists,
and foreign relations including dealings with Eurovision
and Nordvision. It is stressed, however, that these
common services should mainly have a technical, commercial
and co-ordination function and that they should not
otherwise limit the freedom of the programme units.

Certain co-ordination procedures have also been
included in the directives, but these are limited to the
organisation of transmission time for major programme
categories and to political programmes, particularly in
connection with elections.

Within this framework laid down by the authorities,
the corporation is free to adopt its own organisation.

3 The rules concerning the composition of the Board of
Governors are incorporated in the Articles of Association.
The board consists of a chairman and ten members, as well
as ten alternate members. The chairman and half the
members and alternate members are appointed by the government; the other half is elected by the General Meeting.
The board also has two representatives of the staff and
their alternates.

The members of the board, whether appointed by government or elected by the shareholders, are supposed to
represent not primarily the authorities but a wide range
of interest groups, organisations and various popular
movements. Apart from the chairman there is in fact no
member of the board who holds a position in government or
the administration. The composition of the board is generally settled after negotiations between the minister concerned, the political parties and the major organisations
and institutions represented on the board.

Operational

The main principle of the legislation now in force is,
exactly as in previous legislation, that the corporation
should be independent and autonomous at the operational
level.

Financial

The Radio Act itself does not include provisions concerning the financing of broadcasting, except for the
permission given to government in Art. 3 to prescribe fees
for the possession of receivers, subject to approval by
parliament.   The basic financial regulations are in the
Agreement (Art. 3, 12, 14-16).

(b)   With Telecommunicational Authorities

As noted above, the responsibility for the technical part
of broadcasting is divided between the Telecommunications
Administration and Sveriges Radio.   SR has the main responsibility for the long-term planning of broadcasting,
in all its aspects.   The corporation is also responsible
for the technical part of the production of radio and
television programmes, including programme contribution
via inter-urban telecommunication facilities.

The Telecommunications Administration is responsible
for programme distribution and has to provide communication facilities for programme contributions at cost.
Sveriges Radio may, however, within limited areas,
organise its own contribution circuits by radio links.

The Administration is responsible for all radio and
television transmitters and for the telecommunication
circuits conveying the programmes to the transmitters.
Transmission of sound and vision generally takes place via
radio relay links.   Sound radio programmes are distributed
over the same links as television programmes.

As points of daily contact between SR and the Telecommunications Administration, there are a number of
broadcast control centres, one in Stockholm and one in
each of the regional offices.   To solve questions of
mutual interest in the technical, financial and other
fields, there are joint committees at various levels.

The main regulations concerning responsibilities for
co-ordination between Sveriges Radio and the Administration are in an annexe to the main agreement.   These have
been supplemented by further agreements between the two
parties.

The National Board of Public Building is responsible
for the construction of permanent buildings requiring
important capital investment.

(c) With other authorities

The Agreement specifies that educational programming must
be operated in consultation with the National Board of
Education and the Office of the Chancellor of Universities. There are two advisory committees: the School Committee, which is concerned with instructional programmes
in radio and TV for schools, and the Committee for Adult
Education, which provides co-ordination for projects of
special interest to voluntary adult education movements.
Similarly, co-ordination with agricultural authorities is
through an Advisory Committee.

Opinions concerning the efficacy of these formal
structures are divided: it is felt that effective consultation and co-ordination is in fact carried out through
informal working arrangements.

A special case concerns broadcasts of 'societal information' or 'public social information' ('samhällsinforma-
tion'). As mentioned above, the Agreement requires the
corporation to broadcast, at the request of central
government, 'announcements of importance to the general
public'.

The 1969 Broadcasting Inquiry not only made proposals
concerning local radio but also looked into the requirements for an extended use of broadcast media for public
social information. There has been discussion of the need
for more active information activities by both central and
local authorities: in a modern, complex society, it is not
enough for information on the rights and duties of citizens to be 'passively' available; instead the citizen has
a right to be informed in an 'active' way - i.e.
deliberately.

The most controversial proposals from the Committee
concerned the broadcasting of special information programmes produced or commissioned by concerned authorities.
This proposal was heavily criticised; the government also
opposed it because, inter alia, it might jeopardise the
independence and integrity of Sveriges Radio. The
government also pointed to the increase in social information within SR's total programme output, the new possibilities for local social information offered by the new
organisation of local radio and the present informal
arrangements for consultation when required.

5   CONSTITUTIONAL COMPLAINTS PROCEDURE

As mentioned previously, a special complaints procedure
has been established by law. As advance censorship is
prohibited by the Radio Act, a special body, the Radio
Council, has been set up as a public body independent of
SR to ensure that SR exercises its exclusive programme
rights impartially and objectively and also, in other respects, operates the programme service according to the
guide lines laid down in the agreement with the state.

The council only examines programmes which have actually been transmitted. It reports to the Minister of
Education and is financed through licence fees collected
in the Broadcast Fund. The council has seven members,
appointed by government

The council acts either on complaints made to it or on
its own initiative. Its decisions are issued as declara-
tions that the particular programmes are, or are not, in
accordance with the established norms for broadcast
programmes. The council has no other punitive powers but
the Agreement provides that government can make its own
investigation and denounce the Agreement with SR if necessary. The Radio Council has functioned in its present
form since 1 July 1967, and the number of complaints
increased from 179 in 1968 to 653 in 1972.

In 1973 the government investigated the organisation
and procedures of the council. A number of changes were
proposed in late 1974. Although the council should continue to concentrate on control of specific programmes
this should not hinder the council from controlling part
of the total programme output viewed in the light of specific regulations in the Agreement. It was also proposed
that programme output should be classified so that compa-
risons between the programmes controlled and the total
programme output were possible.

Generally, the investigation showed that SR's
infringement of the Radio Act and the Agreement was
clearly below the level which required action against
the corporation.

The investigation summarised its proposed guidelines
for the new control organisation in four main points:

1 The new organisation should be able to exercise more
   surveillance.

2   The work of the council should be limited to
    'important questions', in the first instance to
    matters concerning important principles.
3   The different functions of the council i.e. above
    all the controlling/prosecuting and the judging/legal
    interpretative functions, should be kept separate. The
    judging function should be exercised like trial proce-
    dures which imply the appearance of equal parties and
    oral and public procedures.
4   Complaints which concern the plaintiff should, in
    principle, be dealt with by two legal instances.

The 1973 investigation also proposed a new control organ,
possibly called the 'Radio Ombudsman', to decide on what
control should be undertaken at the council's initiative,
to function as the first instance in all complaints, to
decide independently all matters not seen as having
importance of principle, and to plead in the council on
all matters referred to it.

6   FINANCING

1   Swedish broadcasting is in principle financed through
licence fees; the exceptions are the grants made by the
government for the Overseas Service and Educational
Broadcasting. Certain other SR activities are self-
financed (certain publications, etc.)

    The present licence fees are Sw. Crowns 50 for radio
only and Sw. Crowns 220 for combined radio and TV, with
an additional Sw. Crowns 100 for colour television.

    The Agreement contains a prohibition against commercial
advertising. This principle has been confirmed repeatedly
by both government and parliament, most recently in connection with the new local radio legislation in May 1975.

2   The general procedures concerning the finances of SR
are laid down in the Agreement. According to Art. 3, the
Telecommunications Administration is responsible for
collecting licence fees. Art. 14 states that 'out of the
monies which the Government of Sweden collects or otherwise employs for broadcasting, the Corporation is
entitled each year to that amount which is deemed necessary to finance its operations'.

    In practice, the system works as follows: licence fees

collected by the Telecommunications Administration are
administered through the central Broadcasting Fund.
Every August, the corporation submits an estimated budget
to government with estimates for the budget year starting
on the next 1 July. The decision about the corporation's
budget is taken as part of the total national budget to
parliament at the beginning of the year. The corporation
thus does not itself dispose of the licence fees but
must apply for allocation of funds.

The allocated resources must be used during the relevant budget year; non-used monies have to be returned to
the Broadcasting Fund. The corporation cannot establish
reserves of its own. The only way open to the corporation
for equalising costs between two budget years is a right
to draw upon the Broadcasting Fund. After permission
from government, the corporation can borrow up to Sw.
Crowns 15 million (approx. £1.5 million); the loan has to
be repaid during the following year.

It has been pointed out that this system is not condu-
cive to coherent long-term planning. The corporation's
difficulties regarding reserves and long-term planning
make it very sensitive to sudden cuts in the budget.
The corporation has high 'fixed' costs and a sudden lack
of liquidity hits the only parts in the budget which are
not firmly committed, i.e. mainly certain programme
resources ('uncommitted programme resources'). The economic basis for Sveriges Radio, as for most other West
European broadcasting organisations financially dependent
on licence fees, has changed during the last few years.
On the one hand, saturation levels of receiver ownership
have almost been reached so that automatic increases of
licence revenue can no longer be expected. On the other
hand, the broadcasting organisations have to cope with a
more or less rapid increase in costs and inflation.

Increasing licence fees seems to be politically more
difficult than cost increases in other sectors, but
broadcasting in Sweden is, in general terms, still relatively well-off, since the Broadcasting Fund stands at
some Sw. Crowns 3000 million (approx. £30 million).
However, as SR points out, the authorities have not taken
rising costs into account in their general allocation of
funds to SR. According to SR figures, the monies received
by the corporation have increased by about 6 per cent per
year. But increases in costs have been higher, particularly since 1972/3, when the general cost index rose 8 per
cent and 12 per cent respectively. According to an

estimate by SR, the corporation has over the last three years received some Sw. Crowns 65 million (approx. £6.5 million) less than warranted by the increase in salaries and prices.

Chapter 4

SVERIGES RADIO (SR- SWEDISH BROADCASTING ORGANISATION)

1 GENERAL

There is general agreement within and without the corporation that the basic conditions for broadcasting in Sweden
should not be changed. Freedom from commercial consider-
ations and independence in relation to the authorities
and interest groups, which are the basis of current regulations, are seen as fundamental. The same holds true for
the requirement of impartiality and factuality.

Radio and television are thus seen as having a public
service character: independence avoids pressure from
outside and can provide for new initiatives, and origi-
nality in presentation, as well as variety and diversity
in programme production.

Great importance is attached to decentralisation, both
structurally and geographically. One of the basic
aspects of the 1966 legislation was to confer far-reaching
autonomy on the programme units, while maintaining a central responsibility for co-ordination and for ensuring
that the corporation fulfils its obligations. Management,
i.e. the Board of Governors and the Director-General, has
been described as a group management of a number of
autonomous subsidiaries. Much emphasis has also been put
on geographical decentralisation.

After a recent internal corporation inquiry, the
Director-General outlined guidelines for the continued
decentralisation of Sveriges Radio's activities.

Organisational and technical development should be
designed so as to

1 Safeguard a broadcasting corporation which is in the
   public service and editorially independent - even towards regionally/locally based economic, political and
   other interests.
2 Ensure that planning, decision-making and responsibility are placed, as far as possible, at the same
   level as the corresponding programme activity.
3 Create rational production units, i.e. a balance between staff, technical facilities, local resources and
   programme resources.

Activities and decision-making should be geographically
decentralised to

1 Recognise, harness and reflect regional differences in
   the country.
2 Increase the effectiveness of the public and social
   information available through SR.
3 Strengthen the community feeling within a region or
   smaller area and create interest in it.

2   INTERNAL ORGANISATION

As mentioned previously, the decisions made by the
authorities in 1966 included directives for the internal
organisation of Sveriges Radio, as set out in appendix 1.
The intention was to achieve decentralisation by providing for a large degree of autonomy for each programme
division, including the independent use of allocated
funds. Thus statutorily defined pluralism and decentralised decision-making were to be accommodated within the
corporation which retained overall management and co-
ordinating functions.

Many features of this system were unique; in particular
the establishment of two competing, largely independent
television channels within the same over-all organisation.
Naturally this two-channel TV system has attracted more
public interest than the other aspects of the new organisation.

The two television divisions are supposed to individu-
ally interpret the programme rules laid down in the
Agreement so that their programme output is distinctive
and provides genuine diversity and choice. This competition, however, is meant to be concerned with quality of
programmes and not with viewing figures.

In the public debate this system has been criticised for a number of reasons. The critics have alleged that each television channel has been chasing high audience ratings, that the competition has focused on quantity instead of quality, that despite the absence of commercial interests there has been a 'commercialisation' of output.

In defence of the system it has been maintained that the competition between the two channels has in fact proved stimulating and has had a beneficial effect on the programme output. Viewers are given variety and a freedom of choice which would not be possible if the two channels were complementary rather than competitive. Also, according to a major study undertaken by Sveriges Radio with the assistance of outside mass media researchers, the output has really become more serious as a result of the two-channel system. Thus, if by 'commercialisation' is meant a vying for larger audience figures with 'popular' programmes, this part of the criticism does not seem to be correct.

In another perspective, the current debate about the role of television has been expressed in terms of two conflicting objectives set for broadcasting. It is to the benefit of society that the citizens are well informed and that this information is comprehensive. It is to the benefit of the public that as many of its interests and wishes as possible should be catered for. In this respect experience shows that the entertainment function plays a dominating role, particularly in contrast with societal demands. The mission entrusted to broadcasting by on the one hand society, on the other hand the public, are thus partly irreconcilable, and this issue cannot be solved through any single decision on the relative weight which should be given to various desires and demands.

3   FINANCIAL STATEMENTS

Statements concerning the overall financial situation and the allocation of costs are attached in appendices 2 a, b, c, and 3 d.

4   PROGRAMME OUTPUT

In sound broadcasting the total transmission time has been relatively constant during the last few years: in 1969-70 the total transmission time equalled 17,148 hours

or 328.9 hours per week; in 1974-5 the total transmission
time equalled 19,003 hours or 367 hours per week. During
the same period, the total transmission time in television increased from 57.5 hours per week in 1969-70 to
91.9 hours per week in 1974-5, or approximately 2,985 and
7,787 hours per year.

   Programme statistics for radio and television by
programme category are attached in appendices 3 a and b.

Chapter 5

SPECIAL FEATURES

1 EDITORIAL CONTROL AND RESPONSIBILITY

1 Under the new organisation editorial control and
responsibility has been decentralised and diffused
several levels. The autonomy of the programme divisions
altered the relationship between them and the central
management. But there was also a further decentralisation
of decision-making within the programme divisions. The
most interesting examples of this are the internal
arrangements made by the two TV channels. The attached
charts outline the structure which was originally applied
regarding organisation and decision-making. A descrip-
tion of how these structures work in practice has been
given in a recent study.
   TV 1 is strictly organised along project lines, which
means that all members of the staff are in principle
directly accountable to the programme director. For
purposes of day-to-day production, however, project
groups are formed to deal with individual programmes
or programme series. A project leader, who is
appointed by the programme director is in charge of
each group. Suggestions for programmes and programme
series are submitted by individual members of the staff
or outside persons, scrutinised by TV 1 and finally
evaluated by the programme director in a programme
committee (whose functions are advisory only).

   TV 2 likewise uses a project organisation for the
actual programme work. The main difference as compared
with TV 1 is that the members of the staff are
assigned from the outset to different programme units
and that the planning procedure is formalised with
plenary meetings (for policy issues) and work groups
for evaluation of programme suggestions.

The organisation of the two television channels has become more uniform since 1969. TV 1 has adopted the system of project groups, and the plenary meetings seem to have become less important for TV 2. One major difference remains, however: members of the TV 1 staff move freely between different projects, while members of the TV 2 staff are primarily allotted to a number of different 'editorial offices'.

The organisation of both television channels was in reaction to the departmental system that was in force earlier. Such a system - with department heads, section heads and so on - was thought to lead to stagnation in the programme work for two reasons: first, the difficulty of getting through programme suggestions which the department heads disliked; and second, the difficulties of bringing about co-operation across department boundaries. The new structures were welcomed by the staff, especially because they were thought to widen the scope for employee participation and consultative decision-making, and to afford greater opportunities for self-realisation and job satisfaction   (Lars Furhoff, Lennart Jonsson and Lennart Nilsson, 'Communication Policies in Sweden', Unesco Press, Paris, 1974).

2 Decision-making processes have thus been diffused throughout the corporation but management is still responsible in overall terms and has to bear the brunt of any criticism from outside. The corporation has therefore complemented current legal rules with internal programme rules to be applied by all those involved in programme production. These include general provisions valid for all programme activities such as rules concerning legal responsibility towards third parties. There is also a series of special rules valid for particular programme aspects such as consumer information, political and election programmes, prevention of clandestine advertising, etc.

3 In this context, it is important to recall that parallel to the 'normal' system of editorial responsibility, the special legal provisions concerning liability in broadcasting have a direct bearing on editorial decision-making.

As mentioned earlier, the Broadcast Liability Act makes

a responsible 'programme supervisor' mandatory for each
programme. The intention of the law, confirmed by the
Judicial Ombudsman, is that no programme may be broadcast
without the approval of the programme supervisors, who
are responsible for breaches against the legislation concerning freedom of expression and its limitations (protection of personal integrity, etc.)

4 A further factor relates to the far-going rules concerning 'droit moral' included in the Copyright Act of
1960. In Article 3, it is stated that:
  A work may not be changed in a manner which is pre-
  judicial to the author's literary or artistic repu-
  tation, or to his individuality; nor may it be made
  available to the public in such a form or context as
  to prejudice the author in the manner stated. The
  author may with binding effect only waive his right
  under this section in regard to clearly specified uses
  of the work.

This rule's application to broadcasting has been
tested in the courts. The Director-General had ordered
certain cuts in a programme before it was broadcast, in
keeping with the corporation's obligations under the
Radio Act and the Agreement. The programme producer
sued the Director-General and won his case in the first
instance on the grounds that the cuts had infringed his
moral rights. The Appeal Court reversed the decision but
allowed the case to be brought before the Supreme Court,
which confirmed the Appeal Court verdict without, however, expressing a judgment on the matter of principle.
The task of the Supreme Court had, admittedly, been difficult due to the obvious conflict between two legislative
texts, the Broadcasting Liability Act and the Copyright
Act.

2 RESEARCH

1 The Audience and Programme Research Department of
Sveriges Radio (SR/PUB) was set up in the 1950s; it grew
rapidly during the 1960s and became an independent
department with the reorganisation of the corporation in
1969. The department's aim is to be self-financing and
there is a management committee, which in principle functions as a corporate board of directors. SR/PUB may work
under contract for external clients in the whole field of
mass communications. This facility is also available to

government agencies, interested organisations and
industry and commerce according to special rules.

Generally speaking, applied research is ordered and
paid for by the broadcasting units or external clients,
whereas basic research is initiated by SR/PUB and
financed partly out of funds administered jointly by
Sveriges Radio and the Telecommunications Administration
and partly out of public research funds.

In the beginning, the activities of SR/PUB mainly
concerned the size of the audience, the degree of
interest in various programme areas, the effect of certain types of special programmes, etc. With time the
range of activities widened: lately the research work
has been based on a dialogue between PUB and the units
within the corporation, which has made possible a more
systematic mapping of certain aspects of the mass
communication process.

The overall objectives of SR/PUB are:

(a)   to increase and disseminate knowledge about the
      known and possible effects of radio and television;
(b)   to provide a basis for decisions on questions
      relating to broadcasting at the policy, planning
      and production levels;
(c)   to provide a basis for discussions about broad-
      casting and other mass media within and without
      the corporation.

Research activities are organised through research
groups whose size, composition and guidelines are
decided in the long-term plan, which is revised each
year.

2 The following research areas are considered the most
important:

(a)   The simple 'head-counting type' of audience research
      is seen as providing only insignificant facts with-
      out adequate analysis. Efforts to explain variations
      in public behaviour and use of broadcasting have
      been widened from the study of factors related to
      the output (transmission hours, programme schedule,
      etc.) and to factors related to the individual, such
      as access to the media, the social situation,
      competing activities, etc.

(b)   Investigations commissioned by programme units and
      editorial offices, which are generally tied to a
      specific part of the output as a basis for programme
      planning, or evaluation.
(c)   Longer-term studies on 'information gaps'; recent stu-
      dies and investigations indicate that large groups are
      disfavoured in terms of access to and capability of
      using information in Swedish society. It is still
      not clear how the mass media influence these infor-
      mation gaps. But the media, particularly broadcast-
      ing, have accepted or been requested to assume an
      important responsibility for the information flows
      in society. Other more general investigations con-
      cern the human being as a receiver of information,
      children and the media and the scope and direction
      of the consumption of electronic media. Specific
      projects have investigated local radio, new trans-
      missions and the situation of special groups such as
      Finnish immigrants, adult handicapped and the
      middle-aged.
(d)   The largest research project ever undertaken by
      Sveriges Radio was an investigation of the two-
      channel system in television. The Director-General
      initiated the project in 1973, to study differences
      in programme policy between the two channels, mutual
      influences, criteria for co-ordination and an
      assessment of whether the expectations of this
      system had been fulfilled or not.

3   EDUCATIONAL BROADCASTING

General

Radio programmes have been used in education since the
late 1920s. One of the most important contributions of
school radio since 1945 has been 'English by radio', a
combination of radio and correspondence courses.
Experience from 'English by radio' played an important
part in the introduction, ten years later, of English as
an obligatory subject at the intermediate school level.

Otherwise, radio was used to enrich education and give
it new qualities. In rural primary schools, school radio
relieved isolation and supplied a longed-for break in the
individual teacher's instruction.

In 1964 the Riksdag decided that a special educational
programme unit would be set up within SR (SR/UTB) to

produce radio and TV programmes and programme leaflets for
schools. Programming is operated in consultation with the
National Board of Education. The unit also produces adult
education materials at the request of the two TV channels
and sound radio.

School broadcasting is financed by tax revenue. For
the fiscal year 1975-6 SR/UTB had 19.9 million Sw. Crowns
for programme production and just over 5.5 million Crowns
to cover the transmission costs of the Telecommunications
Administration. The school materials section is self-
supporting, its products being sold to schools at cost.
Turnover in 1973-4 totalled about 10.2 million Crowns.
Adult education programmes are financed from licence fees:
in the fiscal year 1974-5 adult education had a budget
of 2.9 million Crowns.

First and second TRU committees

In February 1967 the Minister of Education asked experts
to examine the use of radio and TV in education and to
supervise experiments in this field. The experts became
known as the Committee for Television and Radio in Education, abbreviated to TRU 1.

TRU 1 directives were characterised by the feeling that
the use of radio and television would offer structural
gains, such as fewer teachers, and higher quality in
education. The TRU 1 production unit started operations
in a TV studio purchased by the state on 1 January 1968.

Until 1972 TRU operated in six different sectors; adult
education, upper secondary school and labour market
training, pre-school education, technology and natural
sciences; social science, and medicine. The three latter
sectors referred to univeristy/college education.

In May 1971 TRU 1 submitted its first report, which
proposed a merger of TRU and the government-financed educational programme department at Sveriges Radio to form a
new organisation.

In December 1971 the government appointed a new commission - the Commission for the Continued Use of Radio and
Television in Education, TRU II. TRU I was to complete
its work with an assessment of its activities to date.
TRU II's task was to plan and supervise work at the TRU
production unit, to propose uses for radio and television

programmes in various sectors of education, and to suggest
a future, more permanent, organisation for the production
of educational programmes. TRU II also examined whether
a system of education patterned on Britain's Open University and other equivalent systems could be applied to
Sweden. This assignment is in its final stages.

For 1975-6, TRU's grant totalled about 20.4 million
Crowns. It also receives 2.6 million Crowns to pay transmission costs via the Telecommunications Authority.

A recent TRU report has again proposed the integration
of TRU and the Educational Department of SR, thus reliev-
ing SR of responsibilities for educational programming
and has stated that this new unit should be placed outside
the Swedish Broadcasting Corporation as an independent
entity directly subordinate to the Ministry of Education.

There is also a suggestion that the proposed new educational programme unit be given special broadcast rights;
the division of broadcasting time should be regulated
through an agreement between SR and the new unit.

The Committee does not, at present, see any reason to
set up special educational channels. However, in view of
the new legislation concerning local radio, the Committee
considers that the question of a fourth radio network
should be discussed. According to the Committee, the
educational programme organisation should be a non-profit
foundation financed by the state to produce audio and
visual programming with or without printed material for
pre-school, school, higher and adult education. These
proposals are now due to be discussed in Parliament.

Chapter 6

RELATIONS WITH OUTSIDE BODIES AND INDIVIDUALS

1 PUBLIC RELATIONS

SR's contact with the public is to some extent dependent
on letters and telephone calls from listeners and viewers.
Recently, however, the corporation has made more planned
and structured efforts to establish contacts with the
public through special meetings, particularly in the pro-
vinces. Both the press and the public are invited to
talk with senior SR staff. SR has also arranged special
information and training sessions of one to two days for
representatives of industry, labour and other organisations.

2 RELATIONS WITH OTHER MEDIA

(a) The press

Since the beginning of broadcasting in Sweden, the press
has been intimately involved in the new medium. It had a
major influence in the Board of Governors and still
retains 20 per cent of the shares in Sveriges Radio and,
thereby, representation on the board.

Compared to the press in other countries, it might be
said that Swedish newspapers devote a large amount of
space to broadcasting. In general, this coverage does
not concern matters of principle but concentrates on
programming and related topics. Sveriges Radio has a
highly decentralised system regarding press relations.
In the last resort responsibility rests with an information department, but in general terms 'information
activities' follow the programme and are thus undertaken
by the concerned programme units. The competition between

the two television channels has also been expressed in
very lively information activities.

(b)   The film industry

As in many other countries, the expansion of television
had profound effects on film production and cinema
attendance. A 1968 Committee in Inquiry into the economic
structure and conditions of the cinema industry reported
in 1973 and initiated considerable discussion. After
further 'arduous negotiations' Sveriges Radio and the
Swedish Film Institute agreed in 1975 to create a joint
fund for financing film production. The fund will be
administered by the Institute. About 70 per cent of the
fund will be used for films to be shown in cinemas. These
films will be available for TV screening after the normal
18-month cinema exhibition period with provision for
individual exceptions. The rest of the fund will be
shared equally between 'short films' (documentaries and
others), films for children (to be shown first on television) and stimulating new film production.

   SR and the Institute must consult each other on the
production of fund-financed films and there is a co-
ordinating committee. The fund began on 1 July 1975 and
the two parties contributed equally to the first annual
budget of Sw. Crowns 10 million. It is foreseen that part
of the sum committed by SR will be reimbursed by the
government.

Chapter 7

FUTURE OF BROADCASTING

The evolution of values and attitudes in Sweden during
recent years caused a more politically orientated public
debate, often with a marked 'radical' flavour and a new
articulation of position and policies in various areas.
This has been reflected, for example, in the adoption of
new public policies in the cultural field and also in the
great attention paid to the media by both public authorities, major organisations and the public. Examples of
recent measures in the media field have already been
mentioned such as the 1975 legislation concerning local
radio and stereophonic broadcasting, the inquiry into the
work of the Radio Council and the proposals for a certain
re-organisation of the complaints procedure, the work of
the Committee of Inquiry on the use of radio and television in education. These activities are, however, only
part of the current official investigation and study of
the media or media-related questions and a number of
changes in broadcasting may well be introduced in the
near future regarding basic legislation, structures and
more specific issues.

1   Since 1970, a Parliamentary Committee has been con-
sidering new legislation on freedom of expression and
freedom of the press. The intention is to replace the
present constitution legislation (Freedom of the Press
Act) with legislation covering all the mass media, including broadcasting.

The Committee has now finished its work and its report
is under discussion. It is interesting to note that it
discussed an extension of the traditional mass media
concept to include new activities, such as street theatre,
demonstrations, etc., but found it too difficult from a
legal point of view to assimilate then under 'mass media'.

2   For broadcasting the most important inquiry is being
conducted by another Parliamentary Committee, on the
development of radio and television, with a brief which
resembles that of the UK Committee on the Future of
Broadcasting. It is expected that the Committee will present its findings in 1976. However, in view of the com-
plexity of the issues involved, the Agreement between the
State and Sveriges Radio has been prolonged for a year
(earliest 30 June 1978) so as to give sufficient time for
dealing with the Committee report. As the report by the
Committee on Educational Broadcasting will not be discussed until after the 1976 elections, it is possible that
the two reports will be dealt with jointly. It therefore
seems improbable that major changes will be implemented
before the end of the decade.

3   Yet another Parliamentary Committee is studying the
finances of the press; the press presently receives
indirect and direct public support of about Sw. Crowns
400 million per year.

4   The concern with economic conditions of the mass
media has also prompted the government to look into the
effects of mergers and concentration of enterprises in
the mass media field and into the use of commercial
advertising in videocassettes and videodiscs.

5   Apart from the above inquiry into videograms, new
technical systems have been given relatively limited
attention. While there has been a certain amount of
public discussion on cable television, no major activities have been undertaken. TRU (the Committee on the Use
of Broadcasting in Education) has conducted, in conjunction with Sveriges Radio, a very limited cable experiment
in Kiruna in northern Sweden. So far, no public policy
has been adopted.

6   The Nordic Council of Ministers is looking into
increased possibilities of trans-border reception of
programmes from the other Nordic countries. Various
proposals are under discussion including the possibility
of making the television programmes of each Nordic
country available to the entire Nordic audience, possibly
with a special joint television channel and possibly
through a joint Nordic satellite system.

If in Sweden comprehensive cultural and educational
policies have been formulated, this stage has not yet been

reached in terms of overall communication policies. However, the intensive work on various aspects of media policies points in this direction. In this context a particularly interesting initiative has been taken by the Secretariat for Future Studies established in the Office of the Prime Minister. Apart from studies on future planning in various areas and on the changing value systems in Swedish society, the Secretariat has also undertaken work on a project called 'Man in the Communications Society of the Future'. In this work particular attention has been paid to information flows in society, the special requirements of disfavoured groups, and the psycho-biological aspects of man as a receiver and transmitter of information. Major research projects are now being planned which will play an important role in the future formation of information and communication policies.

APPENDICES

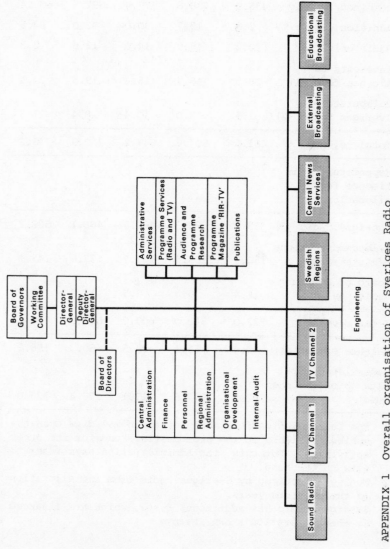

APPENDIX 1   Overall organisation of Sveriges Radio

APPENDIX 2.1 Overall financial statement on broadcasting
for the years 1969-70 - 1973-4 (in million Swedish Crowns)
according to information from the Telecommunications
Administration

Revenue	1969-70	1970-1	1971-2	1972-3	1973-4
Licence fees					
Radio and TV combined/TV only	438.9	458.6	579.4	597.5	605.4
Addition colour TV	2.5	13.7	30.0	52.0	82.5
Radio only	20.2	15.9	14.0	13.5	12.3
Interests on licence fees (1)	18.5	16.7	15.4	19.5	24.5
Reimbursed by Sveriges Radio (2)	1.5	3.0	10.4	18.4	11.5
Total revenue	481.6	507.9	649.2	700.9	736.2
Expenditure from licence fee allocations					
Sveriges Radio (3)	359.7	398.3	462.5	488.1	522.3
Telecommunications Administration	150.9	165.4	137.7	137.6	145.2
Board of Public Buildings	11.4	9.3	9.5	14.9	13.1
Total costs	522.0	573.0	609.7	640.6	680.6
Balance of deficit	-40.4	-65.1	+39.5	+60.3	+55.6
Accumulated surplus (Broadcasting Fund)	242.7	177.6	217.1	277.4	333.0

1 The Telecommunications Administration may draw upon the
monies available in the Broadcasting Fund for its other
activities. For this, the Administration pays interests to the Fund.
2 Monies reimbursed by Sveriges Radio from the allocation
of the previous years.
3 Sveriges Radio has additional costs, which are financed
by the corporation's own revenue.

APPENDIX 2.2 Main activities: allocation of revenue
(Million Swedish Crowns)

	1973-4	1972-3	million Crowns	Changes %
Sound broadcasting	148.6	137.9	+10.7	+ 7.8
Television	386.7	352.7	+34.0	+ 9.6
School programmes	19.3	19.2	+ 0.1	+ 0.5
External programmes	8.2	7.9	+ 0.3	+ 3.8
Publishing activities	24.0	25.6	- 1.6	- 6.3
Total costs	586.8	543.3	+43.5	+ 8.0

APPENDIX 2.3 Sound broadcasting (million Swedish Crowns)

Costs of Sveriges Radio	1973-4	Changes compared to the preceding year
Programme and technical operational costs	81.3	+ 6.4
Regional operations	26.9	+ 2.2
Share of joint central news and current affairs services	6.7	+ 0.5
Share of joint central services	27.6	+ 0.5
Share of social welfare costs in the regular budget	2.8	+ 2.8
Write-off expenditure	6.6	+ 1.6
Restatement of write-off budget	-3.3	- 3.3
Total costs	148.6	+10.7

APPENDIX 2.4 Television (million Swedish Crowns)

Costs of Sveriges Radio	1973-4	Changes compared to the preceding year
Programme and technical operational costs		
TV 1	101.6	+ 5.8
TV 2	100.3	+ 7.2
Regional operations	73.9	+14.4
Share of joint central news and current affairs services	16.6	- 0.6
Share of joint central services	77.8	+ 9.5
Share of social welfare costs in the regular budget	7.1	+ 7.1
Write-off expenditure	27.1	+ 8.3
Restatement of write-off budget	-17.7	-17.7
Total costs	386.7	+34.0

APPENDIX 2.5 Budget 1974-5 according to different kinds
of costs

Staff costs		Sw.Cr. 304 millions
General costs		
Rents, fuel, electricity, etc.	20	
Cleaning, surveillance	10	
Office facilities	5	
Printing costs	12	
Postage, freight, etc.	8	
Telephone, telex, cables	10	
Technical costs (components material, transportation, etc.)	13	
Other costs	<u>11</u>	
		90 millions
Direct programme costs		
Contract fees, etc. for contributions to programmes	32	
Contract fees (news, sports, weather, etc.)	10	
STIM (The Performing Right Society of Swedish Composers)	11	
Royalties to the record industry	6	
Performing rights, film rentals	12	
Other performing rights	13	
Fees (manuscripts, translation, consultancy, etc.)	10	
Freelance (producers, cameramen, etc.)	14	
Social benefits for contributors, free-lancers, etc.	10	
Tapes and film	10	
Other programme costs	<u>42</u>	
		170 millions
Reserves		<u>10 millions</u>
	Part sum	573 millions
Revenue other than allocation from licence fees, etc.		<u>46 millions</u>
	Total net	527 millions

APPENDIX 3.1 Programme statistics for sound radio (programme broadcast hours according to programme content categories (National Services) 1 July 1973 - 30 June 1974)

Programme content	Channel 1 hrs	hrs/w	%	Channel 2 hrs	hrs/w	%	Channel 3 hrs	hrs/w	%	Total hrs	hrs/w	%
Cultural and social subjects												
Science and research	419.7	8.0	7.0	1.5	-	0.1	2.2	0.1	-	423.4	8.1	2.3
Literature and art	618.6	11.9	10.4	4.3	0.1	0.1	4.3	0.1	0.1	627.2	12.1	3.5
Societal subjects	703.3	13.5	11.8				52.8	1.0	0.6	756.1	14.5	4.2
Magazine: culture and current affairs	120.3	2.3	2.0							120.3	2.3	0.7
Religion	386.7	7.4	6.5	0.3	-	-	19.4	0.4	0.2	406.4	7.8	2.2
Total	2,248.6	43.1	37.7	6.1	0.1	0.2	78.7	1.6	0.9	2,333.4	44.8	12.9
Programmes in Finnish	1.4	-	-	412.8	7.9	11.8				414.2	7.9	2.3
Sports												
Sports	30.4	0.6	0.5	112.8	2.2	3.2	326.4	6.3	3.2	469.6	9.1	2.6
Keep-fit programmes	43.0	0.8	0.7				68.2	1.3	0.8	111.2	2.1	0.6
Total	73.4	1.4	1.2	112.8	2.2	3.2	394.6	7.6	4.6	580.8	11.2	3.2
Music												
Orchestral music	119.5	2.3	2.0	273.7	5.3	7.8				393.2	7.6	2.2
Chamber music and instrumental soloists	67.8	1.3	1.1	205.3	3.9	5.8				273.1	5.2	1.5
Vocal music (other than opera)	41.4	0.8	0.7	139.2	2.7	4.0				180.6	3.5	1.0
Opera	0.6	-	-	40.2	0.8	1.2				40.8	0.8	0.2
Music education	213.3	4.1	3.6	1,001.7	19.2	28.5	29.8	0.6	0.4	1,244.8	23.9	6.9
Classical music (gramophone)	226.4	4.3	3.8	583.1	11.2	16.6				809.5	15.5	4.5
Jazz	11.5	0.2	0.2	121.7	2.3	3.5				133.2	2.5	0.7
Other	0.2	-	-	0.8	-	-				1.0	-	-
Total (1)	680.6	13.0	11.4	2,365.7	45.4	67.4	29.8	0.6	0.4	3,076.1	59.0	17.0

Drama												
Plays	200.4	3.9	3.4	1.7	-	0.1	0.2	-	-	202.3	3.9	1.1
Series	76.5	1.5	1.3							76.5	1.5	0.4
Plays for children and young people	13.8	0.3	0.2	0.3	-	-	23.2	0.4	0.3	37.3	0.7	0.2
Other	0.7	-	-							0.7	-	-
Total	291.4	5.7	4.9	2.0	-	0.1	23.4	0.4	0.3	316.8	6.1	1.7
Light entertainment												
Talk shows	105.8	2.0	1.8				136.8	2.6	1.6	242.6	4.6	1.3
Disc-jockey programmes	25.1	0.5	0.4				1,048.0	20.1	12.2	1,073.1	20.6	5.9
Mixed entertainment	76.8	1.5	1.3				971.2	18.6	11.2	1,048.0	20.1	5.8
Jazz							154.3	3.0	1.8	154.3	3.0	0.9
Light music (gramophone)	158.2	3.0	2.6	11.9	0.2	0.3	4,232.7	81.2	49.0	4,402.8	84.4	24.3
Total	365.9	7.0	6.1	11.9	0.2	0.3	6,543.0	125.5	75.8	6,920.8	132.7	38.2
Programmes for young people												
Talk programmes							10.3	0.2	0.1	10.3	0.2	0.1
Mixed programmes	3.0	0.1	0.1				501.4	9.6	5.8	504.4	9.2	2.8
Live music				1.6		0.1	49.3	1.0	0.6	50.9	0.9	0.3
Gramophone							327.6	6.3	3.8	327.6	6.3	1.8
Total	3.0	0.1	0.1	1.6		0.1	888.6	17.1	10.3	893.2	17.2	5.0
Children's programmes												
Talk shows	214.7	4.1	3.6				17.1	0.3	0.2	231.8	4.4	1.3
Mixed programmes	114.6	2.2	1.9				63.5	1.2	0.7	178.1	3.4	1.0
Gramophone	5.7	0.1	0.1	1.3	-	-	96.6	1.9	1.1	103.1	2.0	0.5
Total	334.5	6.4	5.6	1.3	-	-	177.2	3.4	2.0	513.0	9.8	2.8
Various daily magazines	308.6	6.0	5.2				2.1			310.7	6.0	1.7

Programme content	Channel 1 hrs	hrs/w	%	Channel 2 hrs	hrs/w	%	Channel 3 hrs	hrs/w	%	Total hrs	hrs/w	%
Daily new broadcasts and comment												
News, national	101.8	1.9	1.7	24.9	0.5	0.7	5.7	0.1	0.1	126.7	2.5	0.7
News, international	38.3	0.7	0.6	-	-	-	0.8	-	-	39.1	0.7	0.2
Labour market	39.3	0.7	0.7							39.3	0.7	0.2
News comments from the Central News Service	636.0	12.2	10.7	0.9	-	-	149.6	2.9	1.7	786.5	15.1	4.4
Other	47.8	0.9	0.8							47.8	0.9	0.3
Total	863.2	16.4	14.5	25.8	0.5	0.7	156.1	3.0	1.8	1,045.1	19.9	5.8
Sweden, Monday to Friday (magazine)	51.7	1.0	0.9							51.7	1.0	0.3
Other news programmes												
TT News Agency and Stock Exchange	187.7	3.6	3.2	0.3						188.0	3.6	1.0
Other news from the Central News Service	104.2	2.0	1.7	0.4			199.0	3.8	2.3	303.6	5.8	1.7
Weather	264.2	5.1	4.4	0.3			3.9	0.1	-	268.9	5.2	1.5
Total	556.6	10.7	9.3	1.0			202.9	3.9	2.3	760.5	14.6	4.2
Miscellaneous												
Programme presentations, fillers, etc.	183.1	3.5	3.1	157.4	3.0	4.5	55.5	1.1	0.6	396.0	7.6	2.2
Trailers, etc.	0.2	-	-				83.7	1.6	1.0	83.9	1.6	0.5
Total	183.3	3.5	3.1	157.4	3.0	4.5	139.2	2.7	1.6	479.9	9.2	2.7
Adult education												
Language courses				223.1	4.3	6.4				223.1	4.3	1.2
Swedish for foreigners				148.8	2.8	4.2				148.8	2.8	0.8
Other				39.2	0.8	1.1				39.2	0.8	0.2

Total	411.1	7.9		411.1	7.9		411.1	7.9	11.7	411.1	7.9	2.2
Total broadcast time (except sound radio financed through funds from general taxation)	5,962.2	114.3	100.0	3,509.5	67.2		8,635.6	165.8	100.0	18,107.3	347.3	100.0
Sound radio financed through funds from general taxation												
School				290.0	5.6					290.0	5.6	
TRU				55.7	1.1					59.9	1.2	
Trailers	4.2	0.1					2.8	0.1		2.8	0.1	
Total	4.2	0.1		345.7	6.7		2.8	0.1		352.7	6.9	
Total broadcast time	5,966.4	114.4		3,855.2	73.9		8,638.4	165.9		18,460.0	353.9	
Joint broadcasts (2)	62.2	1.2		258.5	4.9					320.7	6.1	
Total broadcast time including joint broadcasts	6,028.6	115.6		4,113.7	78.8		8,638.4	165.9		18,780.7	360.3	

1 Out of which stereo 647.1 hrs/w.
2 Refers to simultaneous broadcasts over two programme channels.
Source: Sveriges Radios Årsbok 1973-4.

APPENDIX 3.2 Programme statistics for television (transmission hours according to programme content categories and channels (National Services) 1 July 1973 - 30 June 1974, repeats included)

Programme content	Channel 1			Channel 2			Total		
	hrs	hrs/w	%	hrs	hrs/w	%	hrs	hrs/w	%
TV financed by licence fees									
General									
Presentation and continuity	72.5	1.4	3.4	47.6	0.9	2.2	119.9	2.3	2.8
Trailers	15.3	0.3	0.7	14.7	0.3	0.7	30.0	0.6	0.7
Public information	5.3	0.1	0.3	7.6	0.1	0.3	12.9	0.2	0.3
Fillers	4.5	0.1	0.2	0.6	0.0	0.0	5.1	0.1	0.1
Total	97.6	1.9	4.6	70.5	1.3	3.2	167.9	3.2	3.9
Culture, Humanistic Sciences									
Religion	44.2	0.8	2.1	3.5	0.1	0.2	47.7	0.9	1.1
Programmes on education	5.5	0.1	0.3	1.5	0.0	0.1	7.0	0.1	0.2
Programmes on literature	3.0	0.1	0.1	9.5	0.2	0.4	12.5	0.3	0.2
Literary programmes	5.8	0.1	0.3	1.6	0.0	0.1	7.4	0.1	0.2
Programmes on art, music, theatre, film	43.1	0.8	2.0	28.4	0.5	1.3	71.5	1.3	1.7
History	19.7	0.4	0.9	12.2	0.2	0.6	31.9	0.6	0.7
Biography	27.8	0.5	1.3	38.2	0.7	1.8	66.0	1.2	1.6
Geography	15.3	0.3	0.7	17.8	0.4	0.8	33.1	0.7	0.8
Other	9.7	0.2	0.5	8.5	0.2	0.4	18.2	0.4	0.4
Total	174.1	3.3	8.2	121.2	2.3	5.7	295.3	5.6	6.9
Politics, societal subjects, technology, economics									
International relations	5.3	0.1	0.2	0.6	0.0	0.0	5.9	0.1	0.1
Politics, foreign	39.1	0.7	1.9	64.6	1.3	3.0	103.7	2.0	2.4
Politics, Sweden	15.6	0.3	0.7	82.7	1.6	3.8	98.3	1.9	2.3
Public administration; environmental issues	11.2	0.2	0.5	22.2	0.4	1.0	33.4	0.6	0.8
Social, legal questions	30.3	0.6	1.4	78.4	1.5	3.6	108.7	2.1	2.5
Technology, industry and communications	10.7	0.2	0.5	6.2	0.1	0.3	16.9	0.3	0.4
Trade and industry, economics	17.9	0.4	0.8	15.8	0.3	0.7	33.7	0.7	0.8

Other	14.7	0.3	0.7	37.8	0.8	1.8	52.5	1.1	1.2
Total	144.8	2.8	6.9	308.2	6.0	14.3	453.0	8.8	10.6
Sports and leisure pursuits									
Sports news	35.4	0.7	1.7	37.0	0.7	1.7	72.4	1.2	1.7
Sports events and sports programmes (other than news)	158.2	3.1	7.5	171.5	3.3	7.9	329.7	6.4	7.7
Leisure pursuits, hobbies	12.2	0.2	0.6	8.3	0.2	0.4	20.5	0.4	0.5
Other	11.9	0.2	0.5	4.5	0.1	0.2	16.4	0.3	0.4
Total	217.6	4.2	10.3	221.3	4.1	10.2	438.9	8.3	10.3
Natural sciences, medicine									
Natural sciences, general	15.3	0.3	0.7	0.7	0.0	0.0	16.0	0.3	0.4
Nature programmes, biology	34.6	0.6	1.6	21.9	0.4	1.0	56.5	1.0	1.3
Medicine	18.3	0.4	0.9	14.8	0.3	0.7	33.1	0.7	0.8
Other	10.0	0.2	0.5	3.1	0.1	0.2	13.1	0.3	0.3
Total	78.2	1.5	3.7	40.5	0.8	1.9	118.7	2.3	2.8
Music									
Instrumental and vocal	39.1	0.7	1.9	21.6	0.4	1.0	60.7	1.1	1.4
Opera, operetta, etc.	10.0	0.2	0.5	8.1	0.2	0.4	18.1	0.4	0.4
Ballet	2.3	0.1	0.1	5.0	0.1	0.2	7.3	0.2	0.2
Folk music	11.3	0.2	0.5	9.3	0.2	0.4	20.6	0.4	0.5
Light entertainment music	29.7	0.6	1.4	18.3	0.3	0.9	48.0	0.9	1.1
Other	7.2	0.1	0.3	2.0	0.0	0.1	9.2	0.1	0.2
Total	99.6	1.9	4.7	64.3	1.2	3.0	163.9	3.1	3.8
Drama and film									
Plays (including filmed plays)	120.8	2.3	5.7	97.6	1.9	4.5	218.4	4.2	5.1
(Produced by Sveriges Radio)	(61.8)	(1.2)	(2.9)	(56.1)	(1.1)	(2.6)	(117.9)	(2.3)	(2.8)
Cinema films	153.9	3.0	7.3	169.8	3.2	7.8	323.7	6.2	7.5
(Swedish)	(18.6)	(0.4)	(0.9)	(32.5)	(0.6)	(1.5)	(51.1)	(1.0)	(1.2)
Short films	23.4	0.4	1.1	10.9	0.2	0.5	32.3	0.6	0.8
Total	298.1	5.7	14.1	278.3	5.3	12.8	576.4	11.0	13.5

Programme content	Channel 1			Channel 2			Total		
	hrs	hrs/w	%	hrs	hrs/w	%	hrs	hrs/w	%
Programmes for children and young people									
Information programmes	58.6	1.1	2.8	93.3	1.8	4.4	151.9	2.9	3.6
Plays, films for children	61.7	1.2	2.9	86.9	1.7	4.0	148.6	2.9	3.5
Cinema films for children	8.4	0.2	0.4	9.0	0.2	0.4	17.4	0.4	0.4
Other	71.2	1.4	3.4	80.1	1.5	3.7	151.3	2.9	3.5
Total	199.9	3.9	9.5	269.3	5.2	12.5	469.2	9.1	11.0
News programmes, other than sports									
Newsreading from the Central News Service	62.7	1.2	3.0	63.8	1.2	3.0	126.5	2.4	2.9
News comments	191.2	3.6	9.0	169.9	3.3	7.8	361.1	6.9	8.4
Special events	26.5	0.5	1.2	22.9	0.5	1.1	49.4	1.0	1.2
Weather	13.8	0.3	0.7	11.0	0.2	0.5	24.8	0.5	0.6
Total	294.3	5.6	13.9	267.6	5.2	12.4	561.8	10.8	13.1
Various magazines (type 'Nationwide', 'Today', etc.)	130.6	2.5	6.2	116.8	2.3	5.4	247.4	4.8	5.8
Light entertainment programmes and series									
Programmes with artists: major shows	39.8	0.8	1.9	36.5	0.7	1.7	76.3	1.5	1.8
Programmes with artists: other	40.1	0.8	2.0	54.9	1.0	2.5	95.0	1.8	2.2
Talk-shows				3.5	0.1	0.2	3.5	0.1	0.1
Contest programmes, quiz, etc.	57.3	1.1	2.7	16.1	0.3	0.7	73.4	1.4	1.7
Request programmes	2.2	0.0	0.1				2.2	0.0	0.0
Mixed programmes	31.3	0.6	1.4	11.1	0.2	0.5	42.4	0.8	1.0
Situation comedies, series	159.0	3.1	7.5	223.1	4.3	10.3	382.1	7.4	8.9
Other	9.9	0.2	0.5	22.9	0.4	1.1	32.8	0.6	0.8
Total	339.6	6.6	16.1	368.1	7.0	17.0	707.7	13.6	16.5
Adult education, SR	37.5	0.7	1.8	36.6	0.7	1.7	74.3	1.4	1.7
GRAND TOTAL	2,111.7	40.6	100.0	2,162.7	41.4	100.0	4,274.4	82.0	100.0

Programmes for foreigners	130.2	2.5	–	–	130.2	2.5
Total production financed by licence fees	2,241.9	43.1	2,162.7	41.4	4,404.6	84.5
Television financed through funds from general taxation						
School TV	344.5	6.6			344.5	6.6
TRU						
Children	23.7	0.5	11.8	0.2	35.5	0.7
Adult Education	39.6	0.7	16.5	0.3	56.1	1.0
Part sum for TRU	63.3	1.2	28.3	0.5	91.6	1.7
Total	407.8	7.8	28.3	0.5	436.2	8.3
GRAND TOTAL	2,649.7	50.9	2,191.0	41.9	4,840.8	92.8

Source: Sveriges Radios Årsbok 1974-4.